FIRST BIOGRAPHIES

Abigail Adams

Cassie Mayer

Heinemann Library
Chicago, Illinois

© 2008 Heinemann Library
a division of Reed Elsevier Inc.
Chicago, Illinois

Customer Service **888-454-2279**

Visit our Web site at **www.heinemannlibrary.com**

Photo research by Tracy Cummins and Tracey Engel.
Designed by Kimberly R. Miracle
Printed and bound in China by South China Printing Company

10 09 08 07
10 9 8 7 6 5 4 3 2 1

10 Digit ISBN: 1-4034-9971-3 (hc)   1-4034-9980-2 (pb)

Library of Congress Cataloging-in-Publication Data
Mayer, Cassie.
  Abigail Adams / Cassie Mayer.
      p. cm. -- (First biographies)
  Includes bibliographical references and index.
  ISBN 978-1-4034-9971-4 (hc) -- ISBN 978-1-4034-9980-6 (pb)
  1. Adams, Abigail, 1744-1818--Juvenile literature. 2. Presidents' spouses--United States--Biography--Juvenile literature. I. Title.
  E322.1.A38M365 2007
  973.4'4092--dc22
  [B]
                              2007009983

Acknowledgements
The author and publisher are grateful to the following for permission to reproduce copyright material: ©Alamy **pp. 11** (Gabe Palmer), **12** (William Owens); ©Art Resource **pp. 10, 19, 23a**; ©The Bridgeman Art Library **p. 9** (National Gallery of Art, Washington, D.C., USA); ©Corbis **pp. 18** (Bettmann), **21**; ©Getty Images **pp. 8** (Stock Montage), **20** (Time Life Pictures), **22** (Win McNamee); ©The Granger Collection **pp. 4, 7**; ©Library of Congress Prints and Photographs Division **p. 5**; ©Massachusetts Historical Society **pp. 6, 13, 14, 16**; ©North Wind Picture Archives **pp. 17, 23b**; ©Shutterstock **p. 15** (Anyka).

Cover image reproduced with permission of ©The Granger Collection. Back cover image reproduced with permission of ©Shutterstock (Anyka).

Contents

Introduction

Abigail Adams was a leader.
A leader helps change things.

Abigail helped change how women live in our country.

Early Life

Abigail was born in 1744.
She lived in Massachusetts.

When Abigail was little, many girls did not go to school.

Abigail did not go to school.

But Abigail's father wanted her to read.

Abigail loved to read and write.

She read books from her father's library.

Marriage

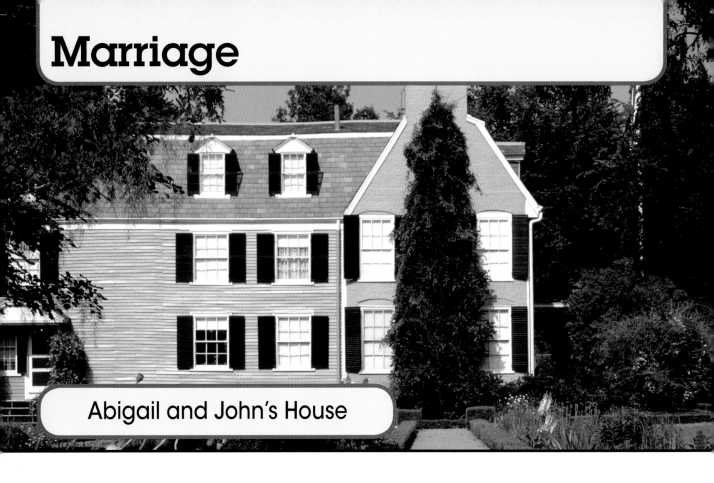

Abigail and John's House

Abigail married John Adams in 1764.

John Adams worked for the government.
The government makes rules for people.

Abigail's Letters

> My Dearest Friend   Bristol May 19 1800
>
> we reachd this place at half after five we found the old inhabitants gone, the new inn keepers name Tombes, the people civil and obligeing. every thing very neat Jackson drove very well. Farmer and Favorite lagg a Traveller & ceasar brisk. I am fully of the mind that a middle size Horse travels with more ease to himself, and pleasure to the driver, we shall get on slowly. I had rather have the Horses want driving than be hickching and flouncing. I hope you will be very careful on your journey not to take cold. I must recommend the warm bath to you once or twice before you sit out on your journey. not hot that will drive the Blood to the Head; but it cleans the Skin & renders the perspiration free. I wish you a pleasant journey. and a speedy return   to your A Adams

John Adams traveled a lot.
Abigail wrote letters to him.

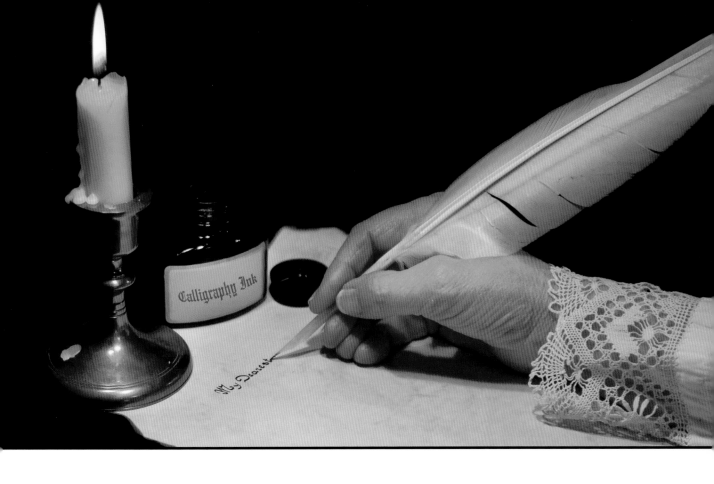

Abigail had many ideas about government. She wrote letters about these ideas.

Women's Right to Vote

> Evils... Then it — I long to hear that you have de — an independancy — and by the way in the new of laws which I suppose it will be necessary for you alike I desire you would *remember the ladies, &* are generous & favourable to them than your ancestors of put such an limited power into the hands of the hands. remember all Men would be tyrants if they do. if perticular care & attention is not paid to the We are determined to

"remember the ladies"

Abigail wrote that women should have the right to vote.

The right to vote is one freedom that
people have. To vote is to help decide
who leads the government.

Women could not vote.

Women could not help decide who led the government.

First Lady

John Adams became president of the United States in 1797.

Abigail became the First Lady of the United States. A first lady is the wife of the president.

ATTENTION VOTERS

Abigail's ideas helped change the
United States government. Women
now have the same rights as men.

Picture Glossary

government a group of leaders who make rules for an area of land

vote tell who you would like to be leader. The person with the most votes becomes leader.

Timeline

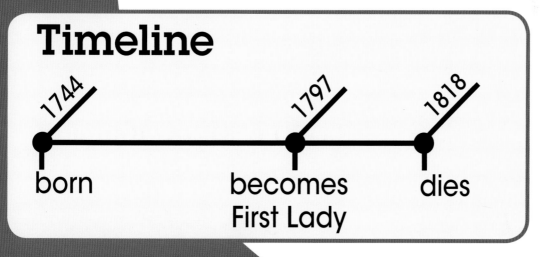

1744 — born

1797 — becomes First Lady

1818 — dies

Index

Note to Parents and Teachers

This series introduces prominent historical figures, focusing on the significant events of each person's life and their impact on American society. Illustrations and primary sources are used to enhance students' understanding of the text.

The text has been carefully chosen with the advice of a literacy expert to enable beginning readers success while reading independently or with moderate support. An expert in the field of early childhood social studies curriculum was consulted to provide interesting and appropriate content.

You can support children's nonfiction literacy skills by helping students use the table of contents, headings, picture glossary, and index.